T.REX

the DINOSAUR with the...

stupid smile

Helen Greathead
Illustrated by Mike Spoor

SCHOLASTIC

Other books in the series:
Iguanodon – the dinosaur with fat bottom

Coming soon:
Stegosaurus – the dinosaur with spiky spine
Diplodocus – the dinosaur with loooong neck

Professor Michael J Benton – dinosaur consultant
Valerie Wilding – educational advisor
Ben Newth – researcher

Scholastic Children's Books,
Commonwealth House, 1-19 New Oxford Street,
London WC1A 1NU, UK

A division of Scholastic Ltd
London ~ New York ~ Toronto ~ Sydney ~ Auckland
Mexico City ~ New Delhi ~ Hong Kong

Published in the UK by Scholastic Ltd, 2003

ISBN 0 439 98285 5

Printed and bound by Nørhaven Paperback A/S, Denmark

2 4 6 8 10 9 7 5 3 1

Contents

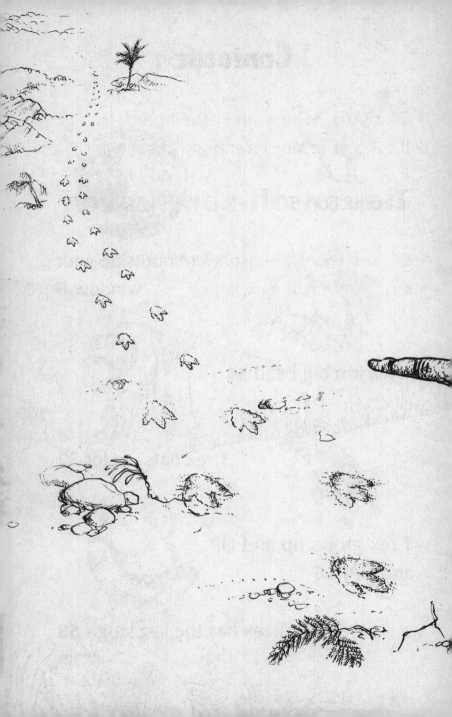

Introduction

Dinosaur names are often hard to say.
It's easier to say Tyrannosaurus rex in bits:

Tie-ran-oh-sore-us rex

Bit of a mouthful, isn't it? Luckily, this
dinosaur has a nickname.
You can call it T. rex
for short.

T.rex outside your window

Imagine this is your house. Your bedroom is here.

You're doing some homework. You look out of the window and see ...

A Tyrannosaurus rex smiling
in at you.

T. rex was probably the biggest, scariest, meat-eating creature that EVER lived!

You can see it had:

• thumping great legs – it could walk a long, long way to find food

• a huge, fat tail – to balance its heavy head and body

• titchy arms – for, er, … well, nobody really knows what they were for.

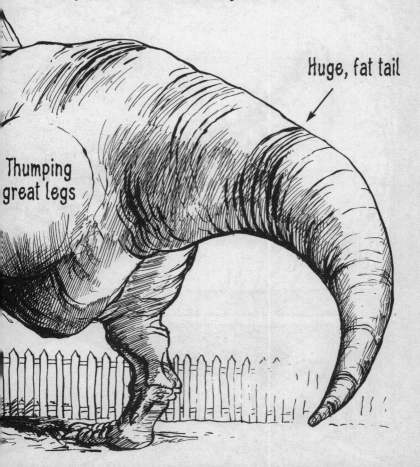

Huge, fat tail

Thumping great legs

And you can see T.rex had a head that was just a bit bigger than you are. You'd fit nicely inside those jaws. So it's a good job you weren't around when T.rex lived!

The smile on its face made T.rex look a bit stupid, but those teeth were no joke. They were huge and sharp, and ready for action.

T. rex is a big head

T. rex might have looked a bit stupid, but it was actually a bit of a smarty pants. T. rex had a great big brain – for a dinosaur. But its brain wasn't all that much bigger than your dad's – take a look:

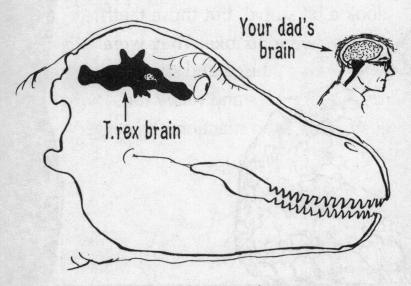

Your dad's brain

T. rex brain

And a brainy dinosaur wasn't brilliant at reading, writing and maths. T. rex needed a great big brain to make it good at seeing, hearing and smelling.

T. rex brain

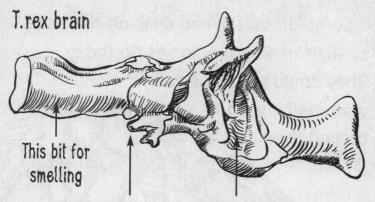

This bit for
smelling

This bit for seeing   This bit for hearing

T. rex carried its brain in its great big
head. And a T. rex skull was so big, it had
to have holes, or "windows" so the
head wasn't too heavy for its neck.

Windows

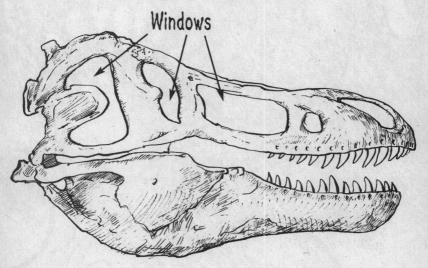

Some dinosaurs had eyes on the sides
of their heads, like horses do today.
They could see if a creature
was creeping up
behind them.

But T. rex had
eyes like yours …

17

… its eyes looked straight ahead.
This meant that T. rex could see
very clearly.
It could quickly
work out exactly
how far away a
creature was. So
when T. rex decided
to pounce … it
didn't miss!

Of course T. rex couldn't read or write,
but scientists know it could hear brilliantly.
And they think it could make noises.

T. rex listened out for dinosaurs it might
like to eat. Vegetarian dinosaurs often
moved about in herds. They called to
each other to keep the
herd together.

One T. rex could hear another T. rex
calling, too.

But even more important than seeing or hearing was smelling. And T. rex had a *very* big nose.

With its incredible nose, T. rex could:
- sniff out creatures that were already dead – so it didn't have to bother killing them

- sniff out creatures that were alive, then kill and eat them
- sniff out T. rexes from another pack – and keep out of their way. They *weren't* friends!

Sniff! Sniff!

T. rexes usually
lived in small
groups, or packs.
The pack liked its
home to be as
stinky as possible.
That way other
creatures would know
this was their land
and *leave them
alone*!
Where did the smell
come from? Well, they
weren't too good at
clearing up. The nest
ponged of wee, poo
and sick!
And that's
not all …

… T. rex had bad breath, too!

Rotten bits of meat got stuck between its teeth. Wherever T. rex went a cloud of flies came, too. The flies fed on the smelly meat. Yuk!

Ever heard of a leech? It's a type of worm that lives on blood. Leeches lived inside a T. rex mouth. Maybe they gave T. rex terrible toothache – because a pterosaur (ter-oh-sore) could poke its beak inside those great jaws to pick out the leeches. And T. rex *wouldn't* bite its head off!

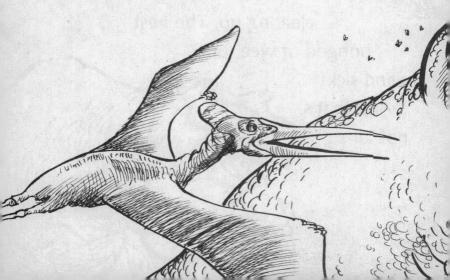

T. rex teeth were this big:

And there were *loads*
of them.

The teeth had edges like a
saw to cut through flesh easily!

Meat stuck to these jagged
edges and didn't slide off again.

The teeth were
shaped like this
across the middle:

They were nice
and strong for
chomping through bones.

They might break on a very
crunchy bone! But each T. rex
tooth had a spare. When one
broke another grew in its place.

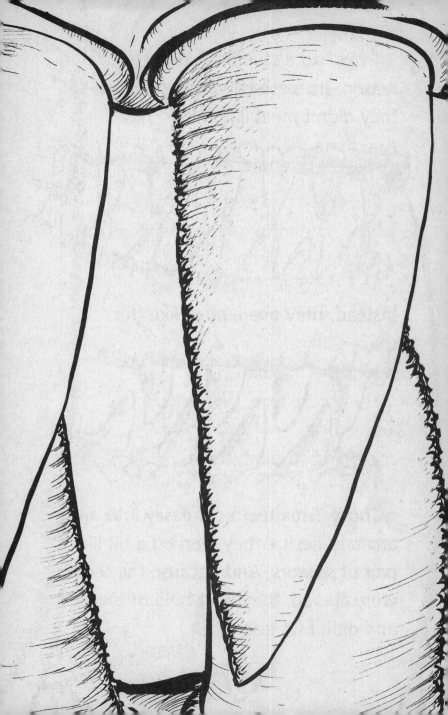

T. rex had a stupid-looking smile for a reason. Its teeth curved backwards, so they didn't meet like this:

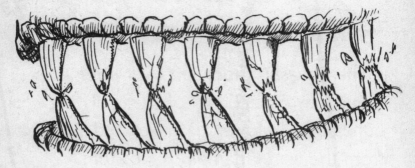

Instead, they overlapped like this:

Those T. rex teeth cut easily into an animal's flesh – they worked a bit like a pair of scissors. And because the teeth were curved, they kept hold of the flesh and didn't let go!

Before

There wasn't much left over after T. rex had eaten a meal. Except the really big bones – and a mush of leaves and shoots from the vegetarian dinosaur's tum.

After

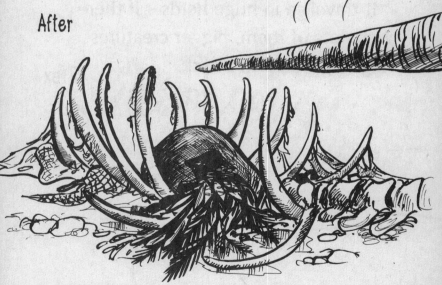

T. rex would eat just about *anything* – anything but its greens!

T. rex eats – a lot

For T. rex, some dinosaurs were tastier than others.

A nice meaty Edmontosaurus (ed-mon-toe-sore-us) was a BIG treat. But it wasn't always easy to catch one.

Edmontosaurus was almost as big and heavy as T. rex.

It travelled in huge herds – if there were lots of them, bigger creatures might not dare to attack.

T. rex

Edmontosaurus

They could call to each other using a special skin pocket on their nose. It blew up like a balloon to make the sound!

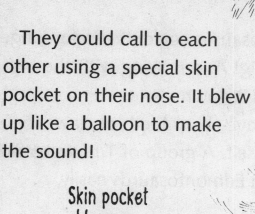

Skin pocket blown up

They could move quite fast – if they had to. But …

... Edmontosaurus couldn't run for long, it was too big! And moving with the herd slowed it down.

It didn't have sharp teeth or claws for defending itself. A group of T. rexes could knock down Edmontosaurus easily.

There were always some weak animals in the herd. They might be sick, or they might be very young – T. rex picked on them first. Why bother running after an animal that could move fast?

A group of hunting T. rexes moved slowly, looking around and listening all the time. But they didn't attack until their leader gave the signal. Then ...

... CHARGE!

One T. rex would run at
an Edmontosaurus with its jaws open
extra wide. It would take a ginormous
bite out of the thin Edmontosaurus neck.
The Edmontosaurus would fall to the
ground quickly. Lunch was ready!

When it came to eating, it was every creature for itself. And there was plenty of fighting over who got the juiciest bits.

But even T. rex wasn't terrifying all the time. It had to lie around for ages letting its food go down. After one Edmontosaurus lunch, T. rex might not eat again for six weeks!

T. rex liked to eat Triceratops (try-serra-tops), too, but they were harder to catch. Why? Because Triceratops *could* fight back. Its head had three long, sharp horns. And T. rex was scared of getting hurt! A wound from one of those horns could kill a T. rex – slowly and horribly.

So … T. rex tried to attack at night, when the herd was tired. At night, T. rex could see better than Triceratops. With luck, it wouldn't be spotted.

Spot the T. rex

But sometimes Triceratops did see
T. rex. Then it would charge with its head
down, and its horns pointing straight in
front. It would aim for T. rex's tummy.
And T. rex, the scariest creature of all
time, would turn and run away!

Triceratops

Some T. rexes preferred to live alone. There was no chance of a tasty Triceratops for them. Instead they might chase a fast-moving Parksosaurus (parks-oh-sore-us). This dinosaur was just a bit taller than your dad. The perfect size to feed one hungry T. rex.

Parksosaurus

T. rex

Different dinosaurs tried different ways
to save themselves from T. rex.

Some tried standing still. They hoped
the patterns on their skin would hide
them.

But T. rex could still sniff them out.

Some tried running in zig-zags. T. rex could move quite fast over short distances, but the zig-zags might confuse it.

And T. rex had to be careful when it ran. Careful not to trip up...

Imagine T. rex is running across a hard patch of ground. It's running as fast as it can.

There's a large tree root lying across its path.

T. rex spots it too late. And falls to the ground …

… CRRRAAASSSHHH!

T. rex was heavy. It held its head quite high off the ground. If it fell, its arms were too tiny to break its fall. It would land on its tummy and wallop its head on the ground, hard. T. rex would almost certainly die!

Life wasn't easy for T. rex. Tripping up was just one danger of being so big. And a smaller T. rex had plenty more to be scared of...

T.rex – grows up and UP and UP

This little dinosaur looks quite cute, doesn't it?

Ahhh!

But don't even think about picking it up for a cuddle! This is a baby T.rex and it can BITE!

When it hatched out, a baby T.rex was all covered in feathery fuzz. It was surprisingly small, and it soon got moving! Baby T. could stand up on its wobbly legs when it was only a few minutes old. And just a few hours later, it would be toddling around the nest.

Grown-up T. rexes would bring food
for the baby. But its teeth were already
sharp and strong. Strong enough
to snap up any small creature
that got in its way.

Snap!

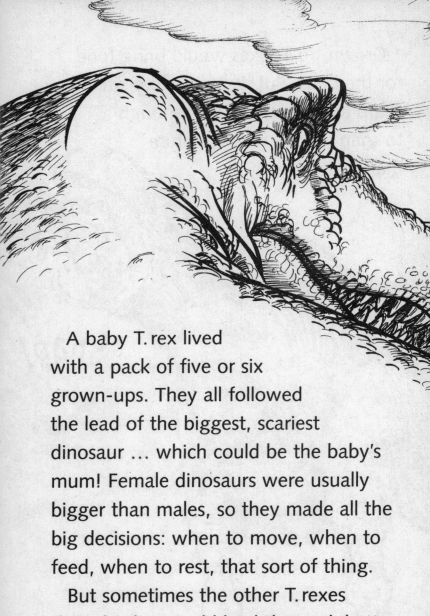

A baby T. rex lived
with a pack of five or six
grown-ups. They all followed
the lead of the biggest, scariest
dinosaur … which could be the baby's
mum! Female dinosaurs were usually
bigger than males, so they made all the
big decisions: when to move, when to
feed, when to rest, that sort of thing.

But sometimes the other T. rexes
thought they could lead the pack better.

The leader had to be on her
guard *all* the time.

Baby T. had to learn to get tough,
quickly.

Here's what Baby T. had to watch out for:
- other dinosaurs might attack and kill it
- it might catch a disease and die
- it might get injured and die of its wounds
- it might even get eaten by another T. rex!

Imagine these baby T. rexes all hatched out together. Having so many brothers and sisters looks like fun, doesn't it?

But one year later, there might be only three of them left.

And a year after that, there might be only one baby left!

And this one's the lucky one! Not surprising they grew up to be so mean, is it?

The two-year-old T. rex wasn't much taller than its dad's kneecaps. And it had already lost all its fuzz. It still had big round eyes and a long, thin snout. And it wasn't big and heavy like its parents, so it could run a lot faster than them. It was ready to go off with the pack.

Eight years old

Two years old

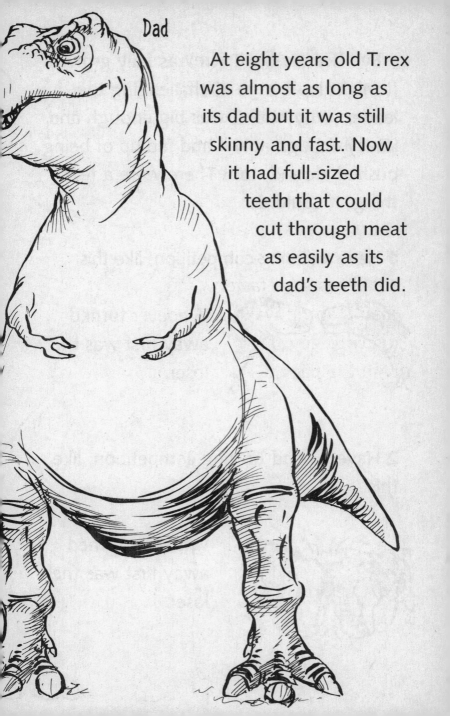

Dad

At eight years old T. rex was almost as long as its dad but it was still skinny and fast. Now it had full-sized teeth that could cut through meat as easily as its dad's teeth did.

By 12 years old T. rex was fully grown. It might have a go at challenging the leader. Why not? It was big enough and heavy enough now – and fed up of being pushed around, too! There were a few things it could do:

1 Have a staring competition, like this:

Whoever turned away first was the loser.

2 Have a head-butting competition, like this:

Whoever turned away first was the loser.

3 Have an all-out fight,
like this:

Whoever *died* first was the loser!

A T. rex fight was not a pretty sight!
One dinosaur snapped its jaws round the
other's neck and kept biting. Then the
rest of the pack got in on the act … and
ate the loser!

So getting to be a grown-up T. rex was tough. But how long would it survive?

It's possible that the T. rexes that did survive just kept growing and growing. As they got older …

… their eyes grew narrower …

… their noses grew thicker …

… lumpy horns grew over their eyebrows (great for head-butting contests) … and they got heavier.

A lucky
T. rex might live
to be well over 100
years old, very slowly getting bigger and
bigger all the time.

T. rex has the last laugh

Scientists know about dinosaurs from looking at fossils. Fossils are bones or traces of dinosaurs, like a footprint or a tail trail, that have turned to rock over millions of years. Fossils can be very hard to find!

There's a place called Hell Creek, in Montana, North America. Over 100 years ago, a dinosaur expert, called Barnum Brown, went there to dig for dinosaurs. And he found the first T. rex skeleton, EVER.

Henry Fairfield Osborn studied the skeleton and called it Tyrannosaurus rex. It means, "king of the tyrant lizards".

A tyrant is someone who is cruel and nasty. So the name suited T. rex down to the ground!

Since
then only
20 T. rex
skeletons have
been found in the
whole world. And only
three of them have
skulls with all the
bony bits in place.

The most famous T. rex
skeleton is called Sue – after Sue
Hendrickson, who discovered her.
Sue's the biggest and the
most complete T. rex
skeleton *ever* found. And
she's worth megabucks!

If you go to America, you can visit Sue
at the Field Museum of Natural History
in Chicago. The museum bought Sue to
attract visitors, and so that its scientists
could study her.

From looking at her skeleton, the scientists have worked out things like:
- how fast Sue could walk
- how well she could smell
- and that Sue might not be a girl dinosaur, after all!

But there's still lots we don't know about T. rex.

No one knows how long a
T. rex tail is. No skeleton has ever been
found with the whole tail in place. And
remember those titchy T. rex arms? They
were about the same size as your dad's,
but the muscles were twice as big!
Scientists know that:

• They couldn't help to catch anything!

Stretch!

• They couldn't reach T. rex's mouth to feed him!

Dribble!

• They couldn't act as legs for walking on all fours!

Oof!

They still don't know what T. rex *could* do with them! But there are new and amazing discoveries being made all the time. Maybe one day soon we'll know the answer.

Dinosaur expert, Jack Horner, has been working on a new dig in Hell Creek. His team have found five new T. rex skeletons. It will take a while to dig them out. But they already think one skeleton is even bigger than Sue!

So even after millions and millions of years, T. rex is still king of the lizards. No wonder it always looks like it's smiling!